A YEAR ON OUR FARM

For my brother Christopher – PM

For the Jackmans, the farm family I know best – AMcL

Omnibus Books
335 Unley Road, Malvern SA 5061
an imprint of Scholastic Australia Pty Ltd (ABN 11 000 614 577)
PO Box 579, Gosford NSW 2250.
www.scholastic.com.au

Part of the Scholastic Group
Sydney • Auckland • New York • Toronto • London • Mexico City
• New Delhi • Hong Kong • Buenos Aires • Puerto Rico

First published in 2002.
First published in this edition in 2002.
Reprinted in 2003 (three times), 2004, 2005 (twice), 2006, 2007, 2008.
Text copyright © Penny Matthews, 2002.
Illustrations copyright © Andrew McLean, 2002.

National Library of Australia Cataloguing-in-Publication entry

Matthews, P. E. (Penelope E.), 1945–   .

A year on our farm.
ISBN-13: 978 1 86291 492 6.
ISBN-10: 1 86291 492 3.

1. Domestic animals – Pictorial works – Juvenile literature.
I. McLean, Andrew, 1946–   . II. Title.

636.00222

Andrew McLean used charcoal pencil, water-colour and pastel for the illustrations in this book.
Book design by Patricia Howes.
Typeset in 18/24 pt New Baskerville by Heidi Goeldi, Adelaide.
Printed and bound by Tien Wah Press (Pte) Ltd.

12 11 10   8 9 10 / 0

Promotion of this book has been assisted
by the South Australian Government
Government
of South Australia   A R T S A   through Arts South Australia.

A YEAR ON OUR FARM

Written by Penny Matthews

Illustrated by Andrew McLean

An Omnibus book
from Scholastic Australia

This is our farm.

And this is who lives on our farm.

SUMMER

January

It's the middle of summer, and the trees in the orchard are loaded with fruit. Jess and I help Mum pick apricots. Georgie keeps eating them!

Maria tries to catch a parrot.
Bad cat!

We put Maria in the hay shed
to hunt mice with Tiger.

There's not much feed left for the sheep. Dad takes us out in the truck to spread hay for them. We check the water troughs, too.

When it's really hot, all the
animals find a bit of shade
to sleep in.

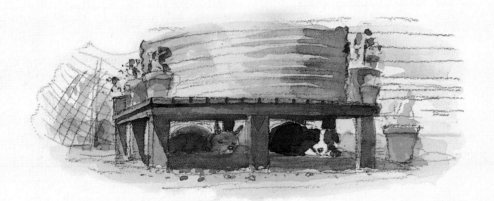

Kelly and Keeper curl up
under the tank stand.

Maria lies under the tomato
plants in the vegetable garden.

AUTUMN

March

We've had some rain! We plant cabbages and carrots. Dad puts up a chicken-wire fence to stop the rabbits from getting in.

Georgie finds a goose egg in the
vegetable garden. It's rotten.
Phew!

Kelly loves chasing rabbits, but
he doesn't catch many.

I think Maria has eaten too
many mice. She is growing
very fat.

Mum is teaching me to milk. It isn't as easy
as it looks. Maria and Tiger come to the milking
shed with us. They know we'll give them a little
drink from the bucket.

Lillypilly loves the new green grass.
She does nothing but eat all day!

Geese eat grass too.

AUTUMN

May

The first autumn lambs are being born. Dad finds a lamb without a mother, and brings her home for us. We call her Daisy.

We put Daisy in a box lined with soft hay. Georgie gives her milk in an old baby bottle.

Maria has three kittens! We call them Socks, Smoky and Little Tom.

May is when we find mushrooms.

WINTER

June

It's cold and wet and windy. Dad mends fences, and we help Mum plant baby trees to make windbreaks.

The chooks don't lay much in winter. Jess and I
have to look hard for eggs. Sometimes they are
still warm.

We've given away Socks and
Smoky, but we're keeping
Little Tom.

Kelly and Keeper live outside all the time, even when it's freezing. They are working dogs, so they're not allowed in the house.

Kelly and Keeper love riding on the truck

… and on the tractor

… and on Dad's motor bike.

Maria and Little Tom are allowed in the house.

WINTER

August

It's starting to get warmer now. Jess and I catch yabbies in the dam. You have to hold them from the back, or they'll nip you.

Dad is crutching sheep. He has to keep their bottoms clean because they can't do it for themselves.

Maria knows how to keep *her* bottom clean.

SPRING

September

Spring time is shearing time. After school, Jess and I go down to the shearing shed to help. Mum brings afternoon tea.

One of our shearers rides
a horse to work.

I wish I had a pony.

Vanessa has gone broody. She won't let us
touch her eggs.

Vanessa has thirteen chicks. Georgie loves to hold them. He says their feet tickle.

There are six goslings down by the dam. Cranky the gander hisses at us when we go near them.

Maria is teaching Little Tom to climb trees.

SPRING

November

Daisy is quite big now. We try to put her with the other sheep, but she cries for us. Mum says we'll have to keep her.

It hasn't rained for weeks, and the dam is going dry. There's only a puddle for Cranky and the gang to swim in.

Three of Vanessa's chicks have died.

SUMMER

December

Dad is baling hay. We play on the bales, and get prickles all down our backs. Georgie gets a rash.

Lillypilly has had a bull calf.
We name it Billy.

We have to water our baby trees
to keep them alive.

Jess and I can't wait for
Christmas. Mum and Dad have
something special for us.
I hope it's a pony!

A whole year has gone past.

And this is who lives on our farm now.